SPORTS GREAT
PETE
SAMPRAS

—Sports Great Books —

SPORTS GREAT
PETE
SAMPRAS

Victoria Sherrow

—Sports Great Books—

ENSLOW PUBLISHERS, INC.

44 Fadem Road	P.O. Box 38
Box 699	Aldershot
Springfield, NJ 07081	Hants GU12 6BP
U.S.A.	U.K.

Library of Congress Cataloging-in-Publication Data

Sherrow, Victoria.
   Sports great Pete Sampras / Victoria Sherrow.
      p. cm. — (Sports great books)
   Includes index.
   ISBN 0-89490-756-5
   1. Sampras, Pete—Juvenile literature. 2. Tennis players—United
States—Biography—Juvenile literature. I. Title. II. Series.
   GV994.S16S44   1996
   796.342'092—dc20
   [B]

                                    95-19101
                                      CIP
                                      AC

Printed in the United States of America

10 9 8 7 6 5 4 3 2 1

Illustration Credits: International Management Group, pp. 9, 14, 17, 22, 24, 28,
30, 32, 36, 47; © Michael Baz, pp. 39, 44, 51, 55.

Cover Photo: © Michael Baz

Contents

Chapter 1

Nobody was expecting much from nineteen-year-old Pete Sampras at the 1990 U.S. Open. After all, he was seeded only twelfth. This placement was well below the top tennis players. Earlier in the year, a hip injury had sidelined him for two months. In June, he had lost in the very first round at the prestigious Wimbledon tournament. That loss had been a big disappointment. Sampras had trained hard and had hoped to do well.

But as the tall, dark-haired player took to the courts at Flushing Meadow, New York, spectators became excited. Sampras unleashed a dynamite serve-and-volley game that flattened his opponents in the early rounds. After Sampras won the third round, someone asked him if he thought he could go on to win the tournament. "Maybe in a couple of years," was Sampras's modest answer.

Yet a few days later he was in the quarterfinals. There, Sampras faced a tough opponent—his former practice partner Ivan Lendl. The steady, hard-hitting Lendl was one of the world's top-ranked players. He was also a three-time U.S. Open champion.

The two players began exchanging strokes in what would be a hard-fought match. To win a match, male players must take three sets out of a possible five. This match lasted five full sets as first Sampras, then Lendl, gained an edge. Finally, Sampras won.

Next came a semifinal match against a former world champion—American John McEnroe. Once again Sampras's booming serve dazzled the crowds and kept his opponent on the defensive. Sampras hit 17 aces. (Aces are serves that are performed so well they are unreturnable.) McEnroe had won the U.S. Open four times before, but he lost this four-set match. At match point (the last point that a player needs to win), Sampras's serve was clocked at 117 miles per hour.

Feeling confident, Sampras went into the final match against a fellow American named Andre Agassi. He had watched Agassi win an earlier match against the defending U.S. Open champion Boris Becker. During that four-setter, Agassi had spent most of his time in the backcourt. He exchanged deep ground strokes with Becker. Sampras compared the play to a long slugging match. He decided not to try to outslug Agassi. Instead he planned to come to the net as often as he could.

Sampras's strategy worked. Up to that point in the Open, Agassi had lost only two sets. Now Pete Sampras won three straight sets to take the match *and* the tournament. His strong aggressive style, including 13 aces, overpowered Agassi. The final score told the story: 6–4, 6–3, 6–2.

When play was over, Pete Sampras had become the youngest man to win the U.S. Open. A sizzling serve-and-volley game had helped Sampras win his first Grand Slam event. Grand Slam events include the Australian Open, French Open, Wimbledon, and U.S. Open tournaments.

When he was interviewed after the U.S. Open final,

Pete Sampras's strong serve was praised after he won his first U.S. Open. Even as a youngster, his strong serve was evident.

Sampras expressed surprise and pleasure. He confessed that he had not been able to sleep the night after his victory. He said, "I couldn't believe it. I was now part of an elite group. My name was going to be on that trophy with guys like Lendl and Becker and McEnroe and Connors and Laver. I couldn't believe that Pete Sampras, a nineteen-year-old kid from California, was going to be on that trophy. Forever."

After the tournament, Sampras found himself in demand for interviews and TV appearances. He was a guest on all three major networks' morning talk shows as well as on *The Tonight Show*. *People* magazine featured a story titled "Float Like a Butterfly, Serve Like a Bazooka: Laid-Back Pete Sampras Blasts His Way Into Tennis History." Sportswriters raved about "Pistol Pete's" rocket serve and all-around game.

People found more to like about Pete Sampras than just his athletic ability. "Sweet Pete," as many called him, was praised for his upbeat attitude and good sportsmanship. There was no shouting, complaining, or racket-throwing from Sampras's side of the court. He was neatly dressed, calm, and professional. Sampras received letters from well-wishers who urged him to stay that way and not let success spoil him.

Later Sampras would tell reporters that he hoped to represent "a nice, clean-cut American image." He said, "I want to be a good role model so that kids will say they want to grow up to be like Pete Sampras."

Since childhood, Sampras has admired the Australian tennis star Rod Laver. Some people call Laver the greatest player of all time. Sampras has often complimented Laver's all-purpose game, gentlemanly behavior, and long career. In response, Laver once said that he was "honored" to be regarded as a hero. He remarked, "Pete wants to bring a bit more tradition to the game. He wants to feel part of the kinship."

Sampras has been called "nice" so often that some people

have complained that he is dull. His late friend, tennis champion Vitas Gerulaitis, once said in his defense, "I'm getting tired of Pete getting knocked for being too quiet. It's just his way of coping. Nowadays, if you don't have some weird slant on your life, people think something's wrong." Friends claim that Sampras is as nice as he seems and has a great sense of humor.

Sportswriters also come to Sampras's defense. Sally Jenkins writes that Sampras may seem detached but that he is actually " . . . a driven, even obsessed young man who is brazenly reaching for a piece of history and doing so with the kind of physical grace and talent that comes along once in a generation, found only in the Lavers, Michael Jordans, Joe Montanas, and Wayne Gretzkys."

Is this guy too good to be true? Sampras insists that he is human, like anybody else. For instance, he says that he cannot fall asleep unless his room is totally dark. He has a fear of dogs and sometimes gets stomachaches when he's nervous. Sampras has struggled with numerous leg and foot injuries, and tendonitis (inflamed tendons). He also wears special supports in his sneakers. Although Sampras usually sticks to a healthy, low-fat diet, he has been known to sometimes "pig out" on fast-food cheeseburgers.

Winning the U.S. Open was a peak moment in a career that was headed for many more triumphs. Within five years Pete Sampras would gain several other Grand Slam titles and more than $15 million in career prize money. But the journey would be a bumpy one—with lows as well as highs. There would be upsets and injuries; disappointments as well as victories. Through it all Pete Sampras would aim to combine his amazing talent with a positive attitude and determination to become No. 1.

Chapter 2

Peter Sampras was born on August 12, 1971, in Washington, D.C. He was the third of four children born to Soterios "Sam" and Vroustrous "Georgia" Sampras. An engineer, Pete's father was then working in the aerospace field for the Department of Defense. At night, he worked in a delicatessen where he was part-owner. Pete's mother was a full-time housewife and mother. The close-knit Greek-American family includes Stella and Gus (who are both older than Pete) and Marion, the youngest child.

Even as a toddler, Pete showed signs of superior athletic ability. Sam Sampras recalls, "When Pete was three, he could throw and kick a ball in a straight line." By that time, the family was living in Potomac, Maryland, not far from Washington, D.C.

The Sampras family did not know much about tennis in those years. But one day, young Pete discovered a tennis racket in the family's basement. He began to spend hours hitting balls against the basement walls. The family got used to the thumping of tennis balls as Pete polished his hitting skills. Stella also enjoyed practicing against the wall. She and Pete sometimes played at the local high school courts.

In the summer of 1978, the Sampras family loaded its Ford Pinto with everyone's belongings, including a pet parrot named José. The family drove across the country to Palos Verdes, California—not far from Los Angeles. Sam Sampras had accepted a new job in the aerospace industry. Sam and Georgia had carefully saved their money in preparation for this long move. The entire family was looking forward to the warm climate.

Tennis is very popular in southern California. There are many public and private courts where people play year-round. Some top players, including women's champion Tracy Austin, also grew up in this area. A number of outstanding coaches also work there.

Seven-year-old Pete Sampras soon became even more excited about the game. His father showed him and Stella a public tennis court near their neighborhood. Watching Pete play, Sam was amazed. He said that Pete hit the ball "so smoothly, as if it was the easiest thing in the world." Pete seemed delighted at the way he could maneuver the ball in different ways.

Soon, both Stella and Pete were spending hours at the Peninsula Racquet Club, which the family had joined. Sam and Georgia got into the act and took turns hitting balls to their children. As Pete and Stella showed real talent for the game, their parents thought about the future. Should the children concentrate on tennis lessons and play in junior tournaments? Or should they have a more "normal" childhood and play for fun? Sam and Georgia decided to keep their children's lives as normal as possible for the time being.

Yet Pete Sampras's talent was undeniable. One day, two people watched Pete playing with Sam in the park. They

Pete's father showed him and his sister Stella a public tennis court by the family's new home in California where the two children could play.

convinced Sam that his son was a prodigy, a truly gifted young person. He deserved to study the game with a skilled teacher. Pete began working on his strokes with Robert Lansdorf. He learned about footwork—the way players move around the court—with expert Del Little.

Lansdorf later said that crowds sometimes gathered to watch young Pete Sampras practice at the Jack Kramer Tennis Club in Rolling Hills Estates. "At age 11, he could pick up volleys at the service line, hit low volleys with all the ease in the world," Lansdorf recalled.

Pete's parents found a new coach who would work with their son from the ages of nine to eighteen. He was pediatrician Dr. Peter Fischer, a part-time tennis teacher. Fischer had never coached before, but he agreed to work with Pete without a salary. In later years, Sampras would credit Fischer for teaching him how to serve and volley and about tennis strategy.

During the years they worked together, Pete's playing style took shape. His coach favored a "serve-and-volley" style. Serve-and-volley players like to serve (hit the ball into the opposing player's service square), then move quickly toward the net. To succeed at this, a player needs a strong reliable serve. Very fast serves and serves that land with a "spin," or bounce, can be difficult for opponents to return. Well-placed serves that land on or near the lines are also difficult to return.

While opponents struggle to return strong serves, serve-and-volley players "rush the net." There, they get into position to volley—hit the ball in mid-air before it bounces on their side of the court. The goal is to put away the ball and quickly score a point.

As he polished his game, Sampras again admired Rod Laver—an outstanding serve-and-volley player. The talented

Australian played from the 1950s to the 1970s. Laver is one of only two men in history to win a "Grand Slam." This means that he won the Australian Open, French Open, Wimbledon, and U.S. Open titles in one calendar year. Laver is the only player to have won it twice (1962 and 1969). In all, "the Rocket" captured two U.S. Open, four Wimbledon, three Australian, and two French titles. Sampras said that he admired Laver because " . . . he could win on all surfaces. He could win any way he wanted, and do it with class."

Other top players have also modeled their game on Laver's. Martina Navratilova, a top female player from the 1970s through the 1990s, once saw Laver play when she was a child in Prague, Czechoslovakia. Navratilova wrote in her 1985 autobiography, "If ever there was a player I wanted to copy, it was Laver."

By this time Sampras was sure that he, too, wanted to be a champion. He later said, "By the age of twelve, I was determined to be a tennis pro." He began playing in United States Tennis Association (USTA) junior tournaments. His ranking was usually in the top 25 U.S. junior boy players.

But Sampras did not always win his early matches. One reason was that he played against boys who were older and sometimes twice his size. These older boys had stronger serves than the "popgun" Pete Sampras had in those days. His coach urged him to play against better players in order to improve. Sampras later said, "My coach and I were more concerned with learning to play well than with winning."

Fischer also urged Pete to concentrate on each point and to avoid idle chatter while playing. According to Fischer, a player needed to make only three kinds of comments on the court: "In," "Out," and the score. Sampras was also told not to show much emotion during a match. The scariest opponents were those who never changed their expression, said Fischer.

Even though Sampras's backhand was his best stroke, his coach wanted him to switch to a one-handed stroke. It turned out to be a wise choice.

At age thirteen, Sampras set an unusual record. He was part of the longest match that had ever been played at the USTA's National Boys' Championships. During the match Sampras suffered a stress fracture of his right wrist. He played the next day but his opponent from the previous match had withdrawn, saying he was exhausted.

In 1985, Dr. Fischer made a major change in Sampras's game. Sampras's backhand had been his best stroke. Now his coach wanted him to switch from a two-handed backhand to a one-handed shot. The two-handed backhand had been popularized by women's champion Chris Evert during the 1970s. It had also been adopted by Jimmy Connors and other male players. Fischer claimed that Pete would be able to increase his reach and get to more shots if he mastered the one-hander.

Sampras was unhappy about the change. His first attempts sent the ball flying off court, sometimes over the back fence. It hampered his match play as well. He lost matches against players he used to beat. Although Fischer reminded his young student to stay focused on the future, Sampras felt frustrated. His ranking went from the top 25 to a dismal No. 56.

Chapter 3

During this period of difficult changes, Sampras looked to his idol for inspiration. He watched films of Rod Laver playing, using the one-handed backhand. He also practiced, hitting thousands of backhands. Finally, the stroke came together, and Sampras began to win again.

Sampras worked on his serve, too. As he grew taller and stronger, his serve gained power. He worked on service placement—putting the serve where he wanted it to go. He also worked on disguising the serve so that his opponents could not predict where the ball was going to land. That way, they could not move into a good position to return it.

To achieve this last goal, Sampras learned to use the same basic motion for all types of serves. As he went into his service motion, Fischer would call out the type of serve he wanted Sampras to deliver—topspin or flat, for example. Fischer later said, "He couldn't have a different motion because *he* didn't know what he was going to serve until I called it."

By age fifteen, Pete Sampras was about six feet tall, one

inch below his eventual height. He made the 1987 Boys' Junior Davis Cup team. His serve had become hard and fast—a cannon. Sampras was building powerful, more reliable ground strokes (forehands and backhands), too.

Sampras tested his skill against top players, including Michael Chang. He had known Chang since they were both seven years old. Chang was now the eighteen-and-under champion. Sampras defeated him during the U.S. Open Junior Boys' Championships. Shortly after that, Sampras came in second at the National Hard Court championships. With his partner Matt Lucena, Sampras went on to win the eighteen-and-under International Grass Court doubles title. He was happy to be doing well on different surfaces—something that he believed was necessary for a true champion.

Winning did not always come easily. Sampras worked hard, especially to improve his concentration during each stage of a tournament. Concentration was a part of his game that he would continue to work on after turning pro.

The Sampras family kept a watchful eye on Pete. Sam and Georgia Sampras wanted him to have a "normal" life and behave well on the court. They did not want their son to be called a "tennis brat" or a "bad actor." This had happened to other top young players who failed to control their tempers. Some threw their rackets when they were upset. Or they shouted at officials when they disliked a call. A few years before, Sam Sampras had seen his son throw his racket at a fence. Sam warned his son that he would have to quit playing if he did that again.

Sampras made a big effort to stay calm, like the players he admired. As he began to win matches, people complimented him on his manners as well as his strokes. He was nicknamed "Smiley" for his cheerful attitude.

By now, quite a few people were paying attention to Pete

Sampras. Sportswriters praised his natural ability and all-around good game. There was talk that Sampras had the talent to be the best player *ever*.

Sampras's sister Stella was also making a name for herself in tennis. At the University of Southern California at Los Angeles (UCLA), she was a leading member of the women's tennis team. In 1988, during her senior year, Stella won the National College Athletic Association (NCAA) doubles title with Allyson Cooper.

By the time Sampras finished his junior year of high school, he faced a tough decision. He and his coach felt that his game was strong enough that he could play as a pro. Sampras loved tennis and wanted to test himself against top players. At the same time, he and his family valued education. His parents did not like the idea of their son being a school dropout. Still, there were ways he could earn his high school degree later on. After much thought, Sampras decided to take the plunge and join the pro circuit. At that point, his world ranking was a lowly 311.

Sampras's first year on the pro circuit, 1988, was not a great one. He did not go far in any of the major tournaments. As for the lesser known events, he did reach the semifinals of one tournament in Schenectady, New York.

Sampras continued to fine-tune his game and to work on concentrating during matches. He got a good tennis workout during one week that he spent at the Greenwich, Connecticut, home of Ivan Lendl. Lendl had become the No. 1 men's player in the world and had three U.S. Open titles.

Later, Sampras said that Lendl "had me biking twenty miles a day, talking to me about discipline and working hard and practicing until I couldn't walk home." Lendl believed that strict training, plenty of sleep, and a healthy diet were

Pete Sampras is not the only talented tennis player in his family. His sister Stella went on to become the winner of the NCAA doubles championship. Pete and Stella are pictured here with their coach, Peter Fischer.

vital to an athlete's success. He urged Sampras to adopt the same habits.

By the end of 1988, Sampras had broken into the top 100 in the world rankings. As 1989 progressed, his ranking edged up to No. 97. That year, Sampras reached the quarterfinals in several events. With fellow American Jim Courier, he won a doubles title in Rome.

By September, Sampras felt ready for the U.S. Open in Flushing Meadow, which is in the New York City borough of Queens. In the second round of the tournament, he found himself pitted against the 1988 Open champion Mats Wilander. It was a tough five-set match. Spectators were thrilled by the series of exciting points. Each man served his best and ran down balls that seemed impossible to return.

In the end, Sampras scored a big upset. As he drove back to his hotel after the match, he could hardly believe he was still in the running. Although he lost in the next round of the Open, his world ranking rose to No. 81.

In November 1989, Sampras and Peter Fischer ended their tennis relationship. Fischer had been frustrated, saying that Sampras should train harder and not be satisfied with second-best. There were also conflicts over financial arrangements, and the fact that Fischer could not travel with Sampras on the pro circuit. For a while after the break, there were hard feelings between the two men.

By 1990, Sampras was working in Florida with a new coach, Joe Brandi, and trainer Pat Etcheberry. There, Sampras often worked out in a hot garage to build his tolerance for playing in hot weather. His routine included riding a stationary bike, lifting 500 pounds with a leg press, throwing a medicine ball around the room, and many stomach crunches.

Sampras had a good start in 1990. In January, he reached the fourth round of the Australian Open in Melbourne. This

Ivan Lendl told Sampras that strict training, plenty of sleep, and a healthy diet were important to an athlete's success. Sampras followed this wise advice, making him an all-around athlete who also enjoyed basketball.

was one of the Grand Slam events that he was so eager to win. Doing well in smaller tournaments was satisfying. But Sampras knew he needed to win the big ones, where the competition was stiffest.

The next month, Sampras won the U.S. Pro Indoor in Philadelphia. His final-round opponent Andres Gomez would go on to win the French Open tournament that May. Sampras was thrilled to gain his first professional title.

Then came a big physical setback. A hip injury kept Sampras out of tournament play for two months. He was not able to train as usual. Even so, upon returning to the circuit, he earned another professional title—on the grass courts in Manchester, England.

Braced by that victory, Sampras prepared for the prestigious Wimbledon tournament, which is also played on grass. Many tennis pros regard Wimbledon as the tournament that they most want to win. Although Sampras did not expect to win his first Wimbledon, he hoped to do well and improve his ranking.

In late June, Sampras joined the world's greatest players at the All-England Lawn Tennis & Croquet Club for the Wimbledon tournament. A flurry of publicity surrounded the players. Famous people, including members of the royal family, watched from the stands as the opening rounds began.

This was not to be Pete Sampras's tournament. Not only did he fail to do well, he lost in the first round. The loss was bitter, and took some time to get over.

Sampras had now been on the pro circuit for nearly two years. While he had played some good matches, Sampras was far from satisfied with his performance. He had yet to win his first Grand Slam event.

Chapter 4

With Wimbledon over so quickly, Sampras returned home to Florida, where he now owned a condominium. After a brief rest, he went back to his training regimen, preparing for the U.S. Open in September.

It was as the No. 12 seed that Sampras took up his racket at the 1990 Open. Not bad, but hardly the standing he was aiming for. Within weeks, life would be very different. Sampras would move up in the world rankings, from No. 81 to No. 6. He would win the U.S. Open, taking home a trophy and a $350,000 check. As a young surprise winner, he would also have an unexpected taste of celebrity.

Sam and Georgia Sampras had not seen their son play his winning final matches. Both found that watching him play, even on television, made them too nervous. So they went to the movies during their son's semifinal match. Then they took a long walk through a shopping mall while the final match was taking place.

During the championship match, Sampras had been surprised that he did not feel more nervous. Instead, as he later said, he had "a great time" on the court. Sampras told reporters, "Today was the best I could possibly play, the best all week and all year."

When the final match ended, sports page headlines carried the news of Sampras's upset victory. "Youngest male champion in Open history," they read, praising his powerful game. Sportswriters marveled at the 100 aces he had served during the tournament.

In an interview, Sampras praised his former coach Peter Fischer. He said that he owed Fischer a great deal for guiding his early career. He and Fischer talked on the phone and began to patch up their disagreements.

Sampras's victory was a thrill for his whole family. Stella Sampras was so excited that she cried on the phone when she called her brother. "I think I was more excited than he was," she said. "You know Pete, he's just so calm and laid back. He just said, 'Hey Stella, How're ya doing?' . . . I just kept thinking about all those years when we played together as juniors and how hard we both worked. Now it had all paid off."

But there was a trade-off. Suddenly Sampras lost his privacy. Sampras was living in a one-bedroom condo in Amelia Island, a resort off the coast of Florida. There he could rest, practice, and play golf. Soon fans began seeking autographs and sending letters. "Your private life isn't private anymore," Sampras told a *Washington Post* reporter.

His seventeen-year-old sister Marion, then a member of the tennis team at Palos Verdes High School, said, "The phone doesn't stop ringing. Mostly we keep the answering machine on." The family finally had to change its phone number.

The callers and letter writers wished him well. People said that they were glad to see a well-behaved athlete on center stage. Sampras has said, "Fans always tell me that they're happy to see a nice guy do so well."

Both Stella and Pete Sampras worked hard on their tennis game as youngsters. After Pete's U.S. Open victory, Stella seemed more excited than he did. Here, they are pictured holding tournament trophies as youngsters, along with their youngest sister, Marion.

Soon, Sampras found himself playing tennis at the White House. President George Bush, a tennis lover, invited him to play doubles. People clamored for interviews, and Sampras made guest appearances on several shows. People learned that he enjoyed playing golf in his spare time and liked music by Cat Stevens, Led Zeppelin, and the Eagles—all popular musicians during the 1970s.

Trainer Pat Etcheberry said of Sampras, "Most guys, when they win, they want to take a break. Not this guy." Sampras was eager to follow his Open victory with some other titles. In December 1990, he won the Grand Slam Cup. This event is only open to the sixteen men who have the best records in the year's Grand Slam events.

After defeating Brad Gilbert in the final, Sampras received a check for $2 million—the largest amount ever paid to a tournament winner in tennis history. His opponent later said that Sampras had played an amazing match: "He is the guy of the future," said Gilbert.

New responsibilities came with earning large sums of money. Sampras's twenty-two-year-old brother Gus had begun traveling with him and managing his business affairs. Pete trusted Gus to advise him on finances and investments for a secure future. While giving his winner's speech after capturing the Grand Slam Cup, Sampras said that he was donating $250,000 from his winnings to the cerebral palsy research foundation. Two of his aunts had suffered and died from this disease, which affects the brain and nervous systems and can involve many handicaps. Sampras continues to donate large sums of money and to play in charity tennis events.

Sampras found that people now expected a lot from him—perhaps too much. He was the man to beat, the one everyone expected to come out on top. The pressure mounted as Sampras began to experience more injuries than usual.

Pete Sampras stands here after a tournament win with his brother Gus. Gus would later travel with Pete and advise him on business and finances.

Much of the time he played with pain in his feet, ankles, and calves. He often had to endure shinsplints.

Plagued by injuries, Sampras could not play in the Australian Open in January 1991. He also had to pull out of other tournaments that he had entered in the early months of 1991. Returning to competition in May, at the French Open, Sampras lost in the second round. The same thing happened the next month at Wimbledon. Of the twenty-seven matches that Sampras had played in 1991, he had won only sixteen. This record was not the kind people expected of a top player. Nor was the record good enough for Sampras.

During an interview in August 1991, Sampras talked about the pressure that he had experienced after his surprise win at the 1990 U.S. Open. He agreed with his childhood friend Michael Chang that being the youngest champion at a major competition was "like carrying a backpack full of bricks around for the next year."

As the fall of 1991 drew near, Sampras prepared for another U.S. Open. In the months prior to the Open, he had strengthened his game and felt good about it. He was serving and volleying well.

Nevertheless, Sampras could not seem to pull together his complete game. In the quarterfinals, he faced Jim Courier, a tough competitor who would often challenge Sampras. This was yet another of the exciting battles that would take place over the years between these gifted young players. Courier won the match in four sets and was praised for his energetic driving performance.

After the match ended, Sampras expressed some relief that the weight of the title was no longer on him. He was widely criticized. Other players and some sportswriters said he lacked the heart and determination of a true champion. "If you can't

Pete Sampras (on the right) holds one of the many trophies he won in the early years. He would go on to win many more titles, but not without some setbacks.

stand the heat, get out of the kitchen" was the message coming from many people.

It was yet another blow in a year of disappointments. Like many young athletes, Sampras had reached great heights without much preparation in how to handle fame and celebrity. People were beginning to wonder, sometimes aloud, what was wrong with Pete Sampras. Maybe his 1990 win had been just a fluke, a fear that haunted Sampras himself for a while. Maybe he didn't have what it takes to be No. 1.

Chapter 5

After his loss at the U.S. Open, Sampras took stock of both his game and his mental attitude. His goal remained the same—to be one of the greatest tennis players ever. With a new sense of purpose, Sampras went back to work. He vowed to become more consistent, more focused, and mentally stronger. He would show the world that Pete Sampras did have the heart of a champion.

That November, a more mature and thoughtful Sampras reached the final of the Association of Tennis Professionals (ATP) World Championship in Frankfurt, Germany. Once again he faced Jim Courier. And once again it was an intense four-set match. But this time, Sampras won.

Late in 1991, for the first time, Sampras joined other American men on the Davis Cup team. During the second six months of the year, Sampras racked up a 36–6 record. He did not play his best in the Davis Cup final in France, however. The American team lost, with Sampras suffering two defeats in singles and one in doubles. France beat the United States by a score of three matches to one.

Again, Sampras made some changes in his training program. Early in 1992, he began working with a new coach, Tim Gullikson. Gullikson, a former player, was known as a great tactician (someone who understands and uses good strategies). Gullikson also had a vast knowledge of tennis. Tim and his twin brother, Tom, had played on the pro circuit during the 1970s.

Gullikson was convinced Sampras could be No. 1. In his view Sampras needed to perfect his ground strokes. They should be equal to his serve and volley. "He's got so much talent," Gullikson once said. "It gives him a lot of choices. Sometimes too many." Like other coaches, Gullikson found that Sampras was willing to change and grow as a player. "Sweet Pete" quickly learned new techniques.

An energized Sampras returned to Davis Cup play and scored some big wins. His first-round victories over two Argentinians brought the United States into the next round, by a score of 5–0. Next, Sampras won an ATP tournament in Philadelphia. During 1992, he also served as chairman of the ATP Tour Charities program.

Gullikson hoped that with better ground strokes, Sampras would win more clay-court titles. Clay surfaces play slower than hard surfaces. Players have more time to move into position before the ball bounces, giving strong backcourt players an advantage. During the spring of 1991, Sampras made steady progress on clay. He advanced in two clay-court tournaments, reaching the final in Atlanta and the quarterfinals of the French Open.

In June, Sampras again set his sights on Wimbledon. Playing consistently well, he reached the quarterfinals. There, he found himself opposite the 1991 champion Michael Stich. Despite stiff competition, Sampras won in three straight sets. But he had more of a struggle in his semifinal match against

Ever since Pete Sampras (left) was a young player, his coaches found him willing to adapt to any change in coaching style. In 1992, Sampras began to work with Tim Gullikson who was convinced he could help Pete Sampras become No. 1.

Croation Goran Ivanisevic. In this battle between two fine servers, Ivanisevic came out on top.

The pain of losing another Wimbledon eased somewhat when Sampras earned his first clay-court victory in Austria. After that win, he collected two hard-court titles, one in Cincinnati, Ohio, and the other in Indianapolis, Indiana.

Although Sampras had been playing well on different court surfaces that year, clay was his undoing again at the Summer Olympics. Representing the United States in Barcelona, Spain, Sampras lost in the third round of the men's singles competition. He and Jim Courier teamed up for the doubles competition. They lost to a Spanish team, after having led the match 2 sets to 0.

It was a tougher, more determined Sampras who arrived at the 1992 U.S. Open. It had been two years since he had won a Grand Slam title. Playing smart, strong tennis, Sampras reached the semifinals.

There he faced Courier, who was seeded first and expected to win. After defeating Courier in 3 sets, Sampras was in the final—his first U.S. Open final since he had won the 1990 title. Luck was not with him. That weekend, he developed a severe stomach virus and required medical care, including intravenous fluids.

Despite his illness, Sampras took to the courts against Sweden's Stefan Edberg, the defending U.S. Open champion. He won the first set, 6–3, but lost the next two—one in a tiebreaker. A tiebreaker is a special short game played when a set score is tied at 6–6. By the fourth set, Sampras looked weak. Edberg won, 6–2, for the match and the title.

In December, Sampras returned to Davis Cup play, teaming up with John McEnroe in the final against Switzerland. Recalling his losses in 1991 Davis Cup matches, Sampras was more eager than ever to win. The match began badly. After tying 6–6, in the first two sets, Sampras and McEnroe lost both sets in tiebreakers.

Down two sets to none, the American doubles team launched a brilliant turnaround. Sampras and McEnroe won the next three sets to take the match. Sampras later called two of those sets the best doubles he had ever played.

All in all, 1992 was a decent—if not spectacular—year. Sampras had captured five titles and won seventy matches—more than any other male pro. His earnings topped $1.5 million. For a while, he had been ranked No. 2. But Sampras's defeats in all of the Grand Slam events nagged at him.

His game seemed to be on the upswing as 1993 began. In January, he reached the semifinals of the Australian Open. That April, he reached the semifinals at the Japan Open, held in Tokyo. He also rose to No. 1 in the rankings, ahead of Jim Courier. There was much debate in tennis circles over who was the better player, Sampras or Courier. Some people said that Courier deserved the No. 1 spot. They argued that Pete Sampras had not won a major tournament for nearly two years.

Sampras played well in the World Team Cup championships in May, helping the United States to capture the Cup. But on clay courts again at the French Open, he lost in the quarterfinals. Once more people took aim at his No. 1 ranking. Sportswriters said that a victory at Wimbledon would prove that he deserved that position.

Sampras felt the pressure as he headed to the All-England Tennis Club that June. Wimbledon was the tournament he most wanted to win but never had. He had been working to strengthen his return of serve. He and Gullikson thought that the return was key to winning the title. Sampras would later say of this effort, "The return of serve—that's what the past

Here, Sampras eagerly awaits the serve. He knew he had to return the serve well during the entire two weeks' worth of play at Wimbledon in 1993.

champions Agassi, Becker, Edberg, they do real well, and I had to do it real well for two weeks."

During the week before Wimbledon, Sampras was invited to play tennis at singer Elton John's estate in Windsor, near London. A few days before the tournament, he felt the pangs of tendonitis in his right shoulder—his serving arm. A trainer worked on his shoulder so that he would be able to play.

Wimbledon was celebrating its one-hundredth anniversary, and the tournament began in a festive mood. The opening rounds went well for Sampras. The weather there, often rainy and damp, stayed clear throughout the tournament. This allowed the grass courts to dry out a bit, making them a faster surface. During his third-round match, Sampras suffered from a nosebleed, but did not let it hurt the game.

In the fourth round, Sampras played Great Britain's Andrew Foster. The crowds wanted Foster, the last Brit left in the tournament, to win. They cheered loudly for Foster and were hostile to Sampras—who won the match. Sampras met more hostility in the quarterfinals against former Wimbledon winner, and crowd favorite, Andre Agassi. From the stands, most of the spectators rooted for Agassi. Agassi's friend, singer-actress Barbra Streisand, clapped whenever Sampras lost a point. However, among Sampras's fans was someone who was very special in his life. She was law student Delaina Mulcahy, whom he had met late in 1990. The two had been dating for more than two years.

His shoulder aching, Sampras asked that a trainer massage it briefly during the fifth set. He gained an edge by breaking Agassi's serve twice, putting Agassi behind four games to two. Holding his own serve, Sampras closed out the match: 6–2, 6–2, 3–6, 3–6, 6–4.

Sampras was on his way to the semifinals. That match, against Boris Becker, was easier than the one against Agassi.

Becker had survived a long tiring quarterfinal match. Even so, he hit some amazing shots. Sampras's serve, however, sizzled. Becker later commented that the second serves were so good (clocked around 97 mph) that they were like first serves (clocked at around 120 mph). After winning—7–6, 6–4, 6–4—Sampras was in the final.

His opponent, the winner of the other men's semifinal match, would be none other than Jim Courier. Suspense mounted as people placed bets on who would win this All-American final, the first since 1984. Knowing these two players, it was sure to be an electrifying match.

Chapter 6

On the Fourth of July, spectators began filling the stands at Centre Court. They were there to watch the men ranked No. 1 and No. 2 in the world slug it out for the top position.

From the start, Sampras saw that winning this Wimbledon would be tough. Each of the first two sets went to tiebreakers. Sampras squeaked by with scores of 7–6 both times. But Courier fought back to win the third set, 6–3. Sampras seemed tired and he made some careless shots.

After losing the third set, Sampras thundered back. Patiently hitting ground strokes, he won a long baseline rally to gain a 4–2 lead in the fourth set. By that time, he needed an ice pack to ease the soreness in his neck. The fourth set went back and forth. First one player then the other won a game.

Sampras later said that he had forced himself to be calm as he stood waiting to return a serve during the eighth game, which he lost. Courier sensed that Sampras was getting tired. Yet Sampras kept serving brilliantly. "When you serve at 125 miles per hour, you don't need to move much," Courier later said. A reporter watching the match wrote that Sampras's serve "burned the lines." In all, he served 22 aces during the exciting match.

At match point, on the brink of victory, Sampras did a deep knee bend to relax. Courier won the point, and Sampras fought back for another match point. This time the point went his way. He won: 7–6, 7–6, 3–6, 6–3.

Later Sampras would describe that moment of victory as " . . . kind of a blur. It all happened so fast, and the next thing you know, you've won Wimbledon." As Sampras rejoiced, the crowds finally gave him some well-earned applause.

However, some people labeled the new champion as too quiet. "Pete's a Bore," claimed one newspaper headline. Sampras tried to take this in stride. He said, "I let my racquet do the talking. . . . I just go out and win tennis matches." But he did show his sense of humor. When someone told him that Diana, Princess of Wales, had been cheering for him, he joked, "Maybe she has a crush on me."

Some journalists defended Sampras. *Tennis* magazine writer John Feinstein said that it was ridiculous to knock an athlete for being well-mannered. Sampras is "exactly the kind of young man you would want your son to grow up to be," Feinstein wrote.

Besides pride in his achievement, Sampras felt relief. His victory at Wimbledon would end the arguments over his No. 1 ranking—at least for a while. He had needed a big win and he knew it. Sampras admitted, "A loss would have been devastating. Maybe career-threatening."

After the tournament Sampras seemed more confident. His coach Tim Gullikson remarked, "Winning Wimbledon confirmed something he already believed, but until you actually do it, it's all speculation. Now he's increased his own expectation level. He's got the belief that he can do anything with his tennis."

Pete Sampras, taking a rare moment to relax off the court, is often labeled as being too quiet. Sampras learned from his coach as a young boy that the scariest opponents are the ones who never change their expression.

Tennis legend Jack Kramer commented, "Pete's got the most talent, the best equipment. And now he's concentrating better because he's finally found a reason to win. The reason is he finally hates to lose."

After the strain of Wimbledon, Sampras's game slipped for a few weeks. He lost some tournaments in the early rounds. During the late summer, he lost the U.S. Men's Hard Court title in Indianapolis. Courier jumped to the top spot, while Sampras slid to No. 2.

As the 1993 U.S. Open began, Sampras wanted to reclaim his No. 1 ranking. A sportswriter for *The New York Times* wrote that Sampras had "to the naked eye at least, no apparent flaws as he takes aim at the United States Open." He seemed more at ease dealing with the pressure of being a top player.

During the Open an amazing quarterfinal match took place on Stadium Court between Sampras and Michael Chang. Sampras has often praised Chang's fierce competitive spirit. He once said, "Chang is the only player who makes me go for too much and overhit. I think he has more guts than anyone on the tour."

That night, Chang pushed the first two sets to tiebreaks, with each man taking a set. A fast-moving Chang pushed Sampras all over the court, making him hustle for points. Suddenly Sampras took off. The last two sets added up to what one reporter called "an hour's worth of lightning bolts." Tennis writer Peter Bodo said that Sampras began "hitting winners from every position on the court." Although the scores in the last two sets were 6–1, 6–1 for Sampras, the play had thrilled spectators. Some said it was the best two sets of tennis they had ever seen.

Moving to the semifinals, Sampras beat Russian Alexander Volkov in straight sets. His opponent in the final was Cedric Pioline of France, ranked No. 15 and not expected to reach the final. With a powerful backcourt game, Pioline had defeated Courier in the other semifinal match.

Playing smooth, smart tennis, Sampras won the final in three sets: 6–4, 6–4, 6–3. The match took a little over two hours. It was a sweet moment as Sampras accepted congratulations and a $535,000 check for winning his second U.S. Open. The title propelled him back to No. 1.

As 1993 ended, Sampras could look back on a spectacular year. He had racked up eight titles and earned more than $3.6 million in prizes. He also made tennis history by being the first player to serve more than one thousand aces in a year—a total of 1,011.

Sampras headed for Tampa, Florida, where he had bought a house and enjoyed training at the nearby Saddlebrook Club. His home was large and comfortable, though not a huge estate like those of some other wealthy athletes. People sometimes teased him for driving an older car when he could buy any luxury model he wanted. Sampras continued to develop his relationship with Delaina Mulcahy, who was studying law in Florida.

More endorsement offers also came Sampras's way. As he had become a "superstar," he received contracts to appear in ads for tennis equipment, sunglasses, sports clothing and shoes, and other products. He had already earned enough money to live well for the rest of his life. By 1994, endorsements would bring him more than $2 million a year.

But money was not Sampras's major goal in playing tennis. He loved the game, and he wanted to reach and break old records. As 1994 approached, people wondered whether Sampras would win the Grand Slam. He already had two Slam events, Wimbledon and the U.S. Open, under his belt. There were two more to go.

Sportswriter George Vecsey wrote about that possibility.

Pete's athletic ability had always been apparent to his father. It is unlikely, however, that Sam Sampras could have known that his son would someday become the No. 1-ranked tennis player in the world.

He pointed out that winning the Grand Slam was no easy task. There was a great deal of talent in the men's tour. As Vecsey said, "Four tournaments on four surfaces in four climates in one year is a brutal test."

Pete Sampras was still determined to do just that—win four tournaments on four different surfaces. His idol, Rod Laver, had achieved that feat. Hoping to make tennis history and reach his dreams, he looked toward 1994.

Chapter 7

Pete Sampras was still "on a roll" in January 1994. He arrived in Melbourne for the Australian Open, eager to snag his third Grand Slam title in a row.

It was not all smooth sailing for the first seed, however. Sampras played a grueling second-round match against nineteen-year-old Yevgeny Kafelnikov. The talented Russian hit ground shots that whizzed past a surprised Sampras at the net. Many of Kafelnikov's well-placed shots hit the lines. The players started at midday and did not finish until evening. The final score was: 6–3, 2–6, 6–3, 1–6, 9–7, in favor of Sampras.

Sampras went on to defeat Jim Courier in three sets: 6–3, 6–4, 6–4. He was praised for playing an artful game. "Everything clicked today," he said. "The rhythm on my serve was great. I was hitting my groundies [ground strokes] as well as I've hit them in a while." Courier had lost six of the previous seven matches he had played against Sampras. Asked what strategy he might try next, Courier joked, "Maybe break his leg on a changeover."

The night before the final, Sampras and Todd Martin, his

next opponent, ate dinner together. Over pasta, they teased each other and had a good time. Of course, it was quite different on the court the next day. Both men wanted to win. Although Sampras was favored, he did not underestimate Martin. In 1993, when Martin rose from No. 87 to No. 13, Sampras said, "I always believed in him. This doesn't surprise me at all."

On January 30, Sampras won his first Australian Open title by defeating Martin in straight sets: 7–6, 6–4, 6–4. To protect himself from the harsh sun, Sampras had been wearing a baseball cap. It didn't fit well, so he tossed it out before the final. He ended up with the title *and* a sunburn. He was now the first player in nearly thirty years to win Wimbledon, the U.S. Open, and the Australian Open one after the other.

Sportswriter David Higdon wrote in a January 28, 1994 article for *The New York Times*, "Sampras is nearly unbeatable when playing at the top of his game." Sampras told reporters that he hoped to maintain the same level of play consistently for several years, so that he could reach his goal of being "one of the greatest of all time."

For the next few months, Pete Sampras played outstanding tennis and dominated the tour. He proved himself capable on clay as he took the Italian Open title in May. Opponent Boris Becker praised his flawless performance during their final match.

Sampras warily looked forward to the French Open. He told a reporter that he still needed "a bit more time to mature and get more experience" on clay. He said, "I'm getting better, but it is definitely going to be a huge challenge for my game on that surface."

Sampras arrived at the French Open with a record of twenty-seven consecutive match wins. But his streak ended there, as Jim Courier beat him in the quarterfinals. With that

Pete Sampras won his first Australian Open in 1994. He was the first male player in nearly thirty years to win Wimbledon, the U.S. Open, and the Australian Open one right after another.

loss went Sampras's hopes of becoming the first man since Rod Laver to win four Grand Slam titles in the same year.

From the French Open, Sampras went on to Wimbledon. As the defending champion, he knew that many eyes were on him. In the semifinals, Sampras was pitted against Todd Martin. Although Martin had beaten him a few weeks earlier, Sampras took this match.

His opponent in the final was the hard-serving Goran Ivanisevic, whose ranking had risen to No. 2. Some of Ivanisevic's serves had been clocked at 136 mph. The first two sets went to tiebreakers, which Sampras managed to win. In the third set Sampras was clearly headed for victory. He took every game and won the set, 6–0. After the match ended, Ivanisevic could be heard repeating, "He's just too good."

As for Sampras, he was elated to have his second Wimbledon crown. Onlookers had been amazed at his smooth performance. During the tournament, he had lost only one set. And he had lost his serve only three times. Ion Tiriac, a well-known coach, commented, "In my book, Pete Sampras is the best player after Rod Laver. He's the most complete player in the world."

Sampras had not won the Grand Slam, but he was still ranked as the No. 1 men's player. He continued to receive many honors during the year, including the ESPY award (as best male tennis player of 1993). He was voted Player of the Year in 1994 by *Tennis* magazine. And he received the Tennis Award from the Jim Thorpe Association.

Injuries caught up with Sampras during the second half of 1994. He had to miss some tournaments because of painful tendonitis in his left ankle. In addition, doctors found a calcium deposit on his ankle. For two months, Sampras rested, playing only two Davis Cup matches.

Prior to the U.S. Open, Sampras was asked about his ankle

and game. Sampras answered, "I think I'm more or less back on track. . . . I'm pretty happy with the way I'm hitting the ball right now." But he was not in top form that September. At the Open, he had a hard time defeating a low-ranked opponent in the third round. His next match was against an unseeded Peruvian player, Jaime Yzaga. Sampras suffered with back pain and severe blisters on his feet during their three-and-a-half hour match. Yzaga kept him on the run. Down 5–2 in the fifth set, Sampras fought, but was not able to come back. Yzaga won the set and the match.

The eventual winner of the U.S. Open was American Andre Agassi. Like Jim Courier, he had challenged Sampras in a number of matches. Sampras was disappointed, but he knew that having several top players was good for tennis. It spurred the players to do their best.

Sampras had thought he might take time off. But an invitation to play in the Davis Cup semifinals against Sweden brought him back to the court. He won a four-set victory against his opponent in the first round. But the next day, he felt severe pain in his right leg. The problem turned out to be a strained hamstring muscle. Meanwhile the U.S. doubles team lost, giving Sweden an edge. Sampras tried to play another singles match, but pain stopped him after only one set. He was disappointed when Sweden defeated the American team, winning a place in the Davis Cup final.

Although he had lost the U.S. Open, Pete Sampras had a strong enough record overall to remain No. 1 during the second half of 1994. By November, he played well enough to win the IBM/ATP Tour World Championship. Overall, in 1994, he succeeded in defending six of the seven titles he had won in 1993.

Another major title was at stake in January 1995 when Sampras arrived in Melbourne, Australia. He has called the

Australian Open the "hottest one of them all" because of the weather. Remembering his 1994 sunburn, Sampras packed a hat that fit. He told reporters that his New Year's resolution was "to stay healthy all year."

As Sampras entered the third round, his friend and coach, Tim Gullikson, was rushed to a clinic. He was suffering from a heart ailment. In the previous year, the forty-three-year-old coach had suffered several strokes. Now, nobody was sure what was wrong. Worried, Sampras hurried to visit Gullikson after his match ended.

Sampras had a hard road to the quarterfinals. Against Sweden's Magnus Larsson, Sampras was down two sets to none when he staged a big comeback. With determination and hard-hitting strokes, Sampras won this match.

In later rounds, he was visibly upset as Gullikson remained ill. He said, "It just broke my heart." January was turning out to be a stressful month. A few weeks before, his girlfriend Delaina Mulcahy had been injured in a car wreck. She had recovered and was there in Australia to cheer him on.

He faced a difficult quarterfinal match against Jim Courier. By then, Gullikson had gone home to Chicago for more medical tests. Hurting from foot blisters and upset about Gullikson, Sampras burst into tears at one point. The public was moved to see the usually calm Sampras showing deep feelings. Courier was concerned and offered to finish the match the next day. Sampras wanted to go on that day and managed to win in five sets. He later said that crying had made him feel better, after keeping so much emotion inside.

Sampras went on to prevail in a tiring, four-set semifinal against Michael Chang. In the final, he faced the U.S. Open winner Andre Agassi. Each man won one set, then Agassi took the third-set tiebreak. He won the next set and match.

Pete Sampras proves that a player doesn't have to be showy in order to be the best. His quiet and composed ways have led to many victories like this one at the Lipton Cup in 1994.

Sampras had lost his Australian title. Although he had served 28 aces, he lost more points than usual due to errors.

Afterward Sampras called Agassi's return of serve "the best in the world." He said, "I'm not going to make excuses. I did the best I could and lost to a better player." Agassi complimented Sampras, too. He said, "He wasn't the best player in the world today. But the reality is he's clearly ahead of everybody." Andre Agassi had one word for Sampras's serve—"Pow!"

The two men knew that they would soon meet again on the courts. Sampras said that a good rivalry between them would "lift the game." He announced, "I'm up to the challenge. I can't wait to play him again."

After a brief rest, Sampras began preparing for the next competition. There were three more Grand Slam events to go in 1995. This included Wimbledon, where he was the defending champion.

But the Australian Open was not his last setback in 1995. Surprisingly, Sampras lost in the first round of another Grand Slam tournament, the French Open. His ranking dropped to No. 2. Said Sampras, "My whole clay-court season has been a disaster." Then in March, he lost a hard-court title—the Lipton Championships—to Andre Agassi.

At Wimbledon that July, Sampras was determined. Facing three-time champion Boris Becker, he played brilliantly to win four sets. Becker said that Sampras "doesn't have a bad shot in his game." He praised Sampras's behavior on the court and called him "a real nice fellow off the court." Thrilled with his third Wimbledon win, called a "three-Pete," Sampras dedicated it to ailing coach Tim Gullikson.

At the U.S. Open that September, Sampras faced Agassi in a tense, All-American final. Strong serves and volleys brought Sampras the first two sets before Agassi took the third. He beamed as he won the fourth set and his third U.S. Open title. Once again, Sampras was on a winning streak, gathering Grand Slam titles.

Pete Sampras still looks forward to winning the Grand Slam—all four titles in a row.

In 1993, after he had won Wimbledon and the U.S. Open, somebody asked Sampras how he could improve on that great year. "Maybe win them all," he said. Pete Sampras has time to win many more titles, including the four-event Grand Slam that he craves. There will be more chances to test his personal best and challenge the record books.

In the meantime Sampras continues to be himself—quiet, competent, and well-respected. "I know I'm not showy or flamboyant like Andre [Agassi] or Boris [Becker]," he has said. "I don't play to the crowd or joke or smile. But this works for me. I'm not changing for anybody."

When young fans ask his advice, he says simply, "Work hard. Don't do drugs. Stay in school." He encourages young players to enjoy the game, as he does.

Michael Chang admires Sampras's ability to recover after a loss. Speaking of his friend, he says, "Even when he's No. 1, he doesn't change. If everybody enjoyed life as much as Pete, it would be a very happy world."

Coach Tim Gullikson has said, "I wonder if the average fan can appreciate how good he is. He's such a great athlete—raw power, unbelievable footwork, finesse."

Sampras's idol, Rod Laver, agrees. "I think he's an inspiration and a credit to the game. Here is someone who hits a ball 120 miles an hour within a six-inch target time after time. . . . He's just a great tennis player. We should respect that ability and that he's sharing that ability with us."

Career Statistics

Career Winnings

YEAR	TOTAL WINNINGS
1988	$46,053
1989	$157,615
1990	$2,900,057
1991	$1,908,413
1992	$1,995,087
1993	$3,648,075
1994	$3,607,812
1995	$2,647,566*

Year-End Ranking History

YEAR	RANK
1988	97
1989	81
1990	5
1991	6
1992	3
1993	1
1994	1
1995	1*

Grand Slam Victories

YEAR	TITLES WON
1988	None
1989	None
1990	U.S. Open
1991	None
1992	None
1993	Wimbledon, U.S. Open
1994	Australian Open, Wimbledon
1995	Wimbledon, U.S. Open

* As of November 7, 1995

Where to Write Pete Sampras

Mr. Pete Sampras
c/o ATP
200 ATP Tour Blvd.
Ponte Verdra Beach, FL 32082

or

Mr. Pete Sampras
c/o IMG
1 Erieview Plaza
Suite 1300
Cleveland, OH 44114

Index